DISCOVER!

AMERICA'S AMAZING LANDMARKS

THE LIBERTY BELL

By Marie Roesser

Enslow PUBLISHING

Please visit our website, www.enslow.com. For a free color catalog of all our high-quality books, call toll free 1-800-398-2504 or fax 1-877-980-4454.

Library of Congress Cataloging-in-Publication Data
Names: Roesser, Marie, author.
Title: The Liberty Bell / Marie Roesser.
Description: New York : Enslow Publishing, 2026. | Series: America's amazing landmarks | Includes bibliographical references and index.
Identifiers: LCCN 2024059419 (print) | LCCN 2024059420 (ebook) | ISBN 9781978544017 (library binding) | ISBN 9781978544000 (paperback) | ISBN 9781978544024 (ebook)
Subjects: LCSH: Liberty Bell–Juvenile literature. | Philadelphia (Pa.)–Buildings, structures, etc.–Juvenile literature.
Classification: LCC F158.8.I3 R64 2026 (print) | LCC F158.8.I3 (ebook) | DDC 974.8/11–dc23/eng/20250130
LC record available at https://lccn.loc.gov/2024059419
LC ebook record available at https://lccn.loc.gov/2024059420

Published in 2026 by
Enslow Publishing
2544 Clinton Street
Buffalo, NY 14224

Cover Designer: Nicholas Switalski
Interior Designer: Rachel Rising
Editor: Therese Shea

Photo credits: Cover, pp. 1, 12, 15, 18, 20 f11photo/Shutterstock.com; Cover, pp. 1, 3-24 Jeffery Edwards/Shutterstock.com; pp. 1, 5, 7, 9, 13, 17, 21 Oleksandr Poliashenko/Shutterstock.com; p. 4 Sean Pavone/Shutterstock.com; p. 5 chrupka/Shutterstock.com; p. 6 Nordroden/Shutterstock.com; p. 7 Kasbah/Shutterstock.com; p. 9 https://en.m.wikipedia.org/wiki/File:Bellringer1776.jpg; p. 11 https://en.m.wikipedia.org/wiki/File:Arrival_of_Liberty_Bell_in_Allentown_-_1777.jpg; p. 13 James Kirkikis/Shutterstock.com; p. 16 John New/Shutterstock.com; p. 17 Anthony George Visuals/Shutterstock.com; p. 19 Roman Babakin/Shutterstock.com; p. 21 MSPhotographic/Shutterstock.com.

Printed in the United States of America

CPSIA compliance information: Batch #CSENS26: For further information contact Enslow Publishing, at 1-800-398-2504.

CONTENTS

BOLDFACE WORDS APPEAR IN THE GLOSSARY.

LET FREEDOM RING!

Have you ever heard of the Liberty Bell? Today, it's a **symbol** of freedom in the United States. It's older than the country is! However, it doesn't ring anymore. Read on to find out what this bell has to do with U.S. history.

THE LIBERTY BELL IS IN PHILADELPHIA, PENNSYLVANIA.

A SHORT HISTORY

The Liberty Bell was made in London, England, for the Pennsylvania State House in 1752. The bell cracked one of the first times it was rung. In 1753, it was recast, which means melted down and made again.

THE LIBERTY BELL WAS RECAST BY JOHN PASS AND JOHN STOW. THEIR NAMES ARE ON THE BELL. THE YEAR 1753 IS IN ROMAN NUMERALS.

The Liberty Bell was hung in the Pennsylvania State House in 1753. Its ringing called lawmakers to meetings. It was also used to gather the people of Philadelphia to hear news. A story says it was rung when the **Declaration of Independence** was approved in 1776, but most think that's untrue.

RECORDS SAY THE LIBERTY BELL WAS BEING REPAIRED IN 1776, SO IT LIKELY WASN'T RUNG.

In 1777, the Liberty Bell was removed from the state house during the **American Revolution**. The colonists were worried the British would melt it down. It was hidden under the floor of a church in Allentown, Pennsylvania, for almost a year.

Zion Reformed Church, where the Liberty Bell was hidden in 1777

ITS NAME

In the 1830s, the bell got its name. Some Americans were fighting to end slavery. They remembered the words on the bell. They were the first to call the bell the "Liberty Bell." It became a symbol for liberty, or freedom, for all.

ON THE LIBERTY BELL ARE WRITTEN THESE WORDS: "PROCLAIM LIBERTY THROUGHOUT ALL THE LAND UNTO ALL THE INHABITANTS THEREOF."

MORE CRACKS

Some think the bell **developed** a narrow crack in the early 1840s. In 1846, the bell was repaired. Workers widened the crack to stop it from spreading. So, the crack you see today is a repair! But a second crack began after that repair. The bell was never rung again with its **clapper**.

clapper
PASS AND STOW
PHILADA
MDCCLIII

A CLOSER LOOK

The Liberty Bell is large and heavy. It is 3 feet (0.9 m) from top to bottom and 12 feet (3.7 m) around at its widest point, at the bottom. It weighs 2,080 pounds (943 kg)! It's made of bronze.

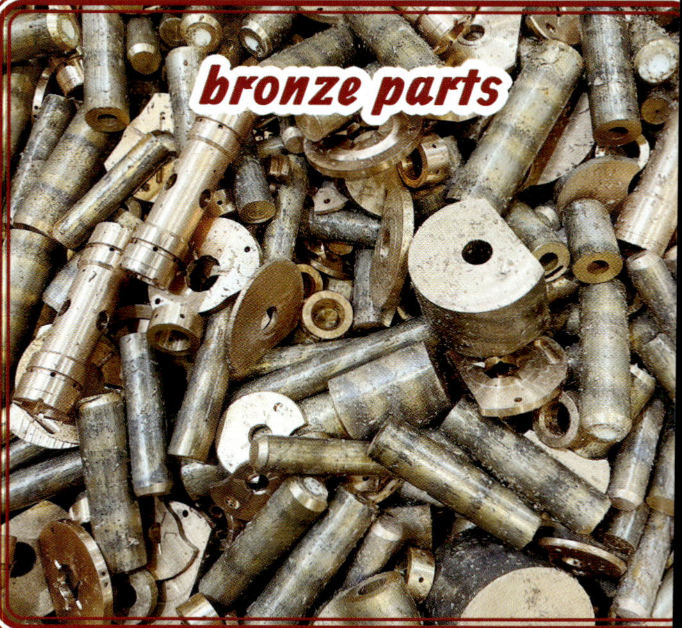

bronze parts

BRONZE IS A KIND OF METAL THAT IS MOSTLY COPPER AND TIN.

VISITING THE BELL

In 2003, the Liberty Bell was moved to a new building in Philadelphia called Liberty Bell Center. It's part of Independence National Historic Park. The state house, now called Independence Hall, is also a part of the park.

Liberty Bell Center

money, stamps, and other important papers. Sometimes, it's still gently tapped during certain **occasions**! The Liberty Bell continues to have a special meaning for Americans.

THE BELL WAS ONCE TAKEN ON TOUR AROUND THE COUNTRY. TODAY, PEOPLE HAVE TO TRAVEL TO PENNSYLVANIA TO SEE IT.

GLOSSARY

American Revolution: The war in which the colonies won their freedom from England.

clapper: A free-swinging metal piece inside a bell to hit its side to make sound.

Declaration of Independence: The piece of writing in which the colonies said they were free from British rule.

develop: To start to exist.

inhabitant: One who lives in a place.

occasion: A certain time or event.

proclaim: To announce something in public.

Roman numerals: Letters that stood for numbers in the Roman number system (I = 1, V = 5, X = 10, L = 50, C = 100, D = 500, M = 1,000).

symbol: A picture, shape, or object that stands for something else.

tour: A trip to many places for a purpose, such as performing music or showing an object.

FOR MORE INFORMATION

Books

Earley, Christina. *Liberty Bell*. New York, NY: Crabtree Publishing Company, 2023.

Wilson, Jon. *The Liberty Bell: The Sounds of Freedom*. Mankato, MN: Child's World, 2024.

Websites

Independence National Historic Park
www.nps.gov/inde/index.htm
See more photos and find out how you can visit the Liberty Bell.

Ten Fascinating Facts About the Liberty Bell
constitutioncenter.org/blog/10-fascinating-facts-about-the-liberty-bell
Some of these facts will surprise you!

Publisher's note to educators and parents: Our editors have carefully reviewed these websites to ensure that they are suitable for students. Many websites change frequently, however, and we cannot guarantee that a site's future contents will continue to meet our high standards of quality and educational value. Be advised that students should be closely supervised whenever they access the internet.

INDEX